William & Catherine

THE ROYAL WEDDING ALBUM

To my mother, and best friend,

Irene Lloyd

with love

This is a Carlton book

Text & design © Carlton Books Limited 2011

itv NEWS © ITV News and ITV News logo are
trademarks and copyrighted. Used under licence from
ITV Studios Global Entertainment Ltd.

This edition published in 2011 by Carlton Books Limited
A division of the Carlton Publishing Group
20 Mortimer Street
London
W1T 3JW

Chapters 1–5 are abridged from *Invitation to the Royal Wedding*
by Ian Lloyd

Printed in the United Kingdom

A CIP catalogue for this book is available from the
British Library

ISBN: 978 1 84732 913 4

itv NEWS

William & Catherine

THE ROYAL WEDDING ALBUM

CELEBRATING THE MARRIAGE OF
HRH PRINCE WILLIAM OF WALES WITH
MISS CATHERINE MIDDLETON

IAN
LLOYD

CARLTON
BOOKS

CONTENTS

Introduction

The Victorian journalist Walter Bagehot wrote, "A princely marriage is the brilliant edition of a universal fact, and, as such, it rivets mankind."

Weddings are not as universal as they were 150 years ago but the one between William Arthur Philip Louis Windsor and Catherine Elizabeth Middleton could be said to be as brilliant as any the Victorians could have dreamed of and was watched by an estimated global television audience of two billion.

Their marriage is in a sense our marriage. We were all invited and perhaps, in this more cynical age, while not everyone would have danced in the streets, many of us watched, listened, downloaded, read or tweeted wedding-related coverage on the day.

Precedent and protocol guided twentieth-century royal courtship. Before marriage, the non-blue-blooded partner was rarely allowed to attend high profile family events or accompany their prince or princess to public engagements. The result was that they had no idea what they were letting themselves in for and went to the altar, as Diana Spencer memorably put it, "like a lamb to the slaughter".

The eight-year romance has given Kate time to grow acclimatized to life in what George VI called "the firm", with every word and action analysed by the media, every new fashion worn either criticized or lauded and every faux pas zoomed in on and highlighted.

This book looks at the personality of the bride and groom; how William's has been shaped by the twin influences of Charles and Diana, and how Kate grew strength from a close knit, middle-class family background in rural Berkshire.

From the beginnings of their romance at St Andrews to coping with its transition into a more public arena, their engagement and its culmination in the wedding that took place, *William & Catherine: The Royal Wedding Album* celebrates the story of the couple who will one day reign as King William V and Queen Catherine.

OPPOSITE: The newly married couple process to Buckingham Palace after their wedding at Westminster Abbey.

1 PRINCE WILLIAM

࿊

June 1982 proved to be an eventful month for the royal family. Pope John Paul II ended his visit to Britain by asking God to "bestow abundant blessings on Your Majesty"; US President Ronald Reagan, on an official visit to the UK, enjoyed an early morning horse ride with the Queen at Windsor; helicopter pilot Prince Andrew was safe and sound in the Falkland Islands as Argentine forces surrendered; and the Queen Mother welcomed home the *QE2* and her 629 troops on board. Meanwhile at St Mary's Hospital, Paddington, on 21 June HRH The Princess of Wales gave birth to a 7lb 1½ oz baby boy.

William Arthur Philip Louis was born at 9.03 pm, 16 hours after Diana had been admitted. A crowd of photographers, film crews and well-wishers built up during the day. When news of the birth broke, so did a rendition of "Rule Britannia", followed by "Nice One Charlie… let's have another one".

A letter written by the proud father a few days later to Countess Mountbatten of Burma, suggests that Charles was still mesmerized by the whole experience. "The arrival of our small son has been an astonishing experience and one that has meant more to me than I ever could have imagined…. I am so thankful I was beside Diana's bedside the whole time because by the end of the day I really felt as though I'd shared deeply

OPPOSITE: On 16 November 2010 Prince William announced his engagement to Kate Middleton saying "We are both very, very happy"; the couple met at university and had been dating since 2003.

in the process of birth and as a result was rewarded by seeing a small creature which belonged to us even though he seemed to belong to everyone else as well!"

Home for the newborn prince was an L-shaped apartment in Kensington Palace, newly renovated by South African designer Dudley Poplak.

With Charles and Diana in constant demand to carry out royal engagements, the baby prince spent most of his day with his nanny, Barbara Barnes, the 42-year-old daughter of a forestry worker who liked her little charges to call her by her first name and who didn't wear the formidable nursery uniforms that would have been a requirement a generation earlier.

William was only nine months old when, accompanied by Nanny Barnes, he joined his parents for their six-week tour of Australia and New Zealand, clocking up more than 30,000 miles of travel. "We didn't see much of him," recalled Diana later, "but at least we were under the same sky so to speak."

Prince Harry was born on 15 September 1984 when William was just two. Any fear of sibling rivalry was quickly dispelled as Diana noted to a friend, "William adores his little brother and spends the entire time pouring an endless supply of hugs and kisses on Harry, and we are hardly allowed near."

Unfortunately the angelic phase was short lasting. By the time he was four William was creating havoc, once trying to flush his father's shoe down the lavatory and another time setting off the alarms on the Queen's Balmoral estate, resulting in police cars hurtling in from Aberdeen to seal off the grounds.

In September 1985, aged three he was sent to Mrs Mynors' Nursery School in Notting Hill Gate where he joined Cygnet Class which consisted of 12 pupils and one detective. After 15 months, the prince moved on to nearby Wetherby School, where he would stay for the next three years. He was noted for his flair in English and spelling and proved he had inherited his mother's love of swimming by winning the Grunfield Cup for the best overall swimming style.

ABOVE: The Prince and Princess of Wales leave St Mary's Hospital, Paddington, on 22 June 1982 with their newborn son, William; the new prince is second in line to the throne after his father.

OPPOSITE: The Queen Mother proudly holds Prince William at his christening in Buckingham Palace on 4 August 1982, flanked by The Queen and the Prince of Wales; the day also marked William's great-grandmother's 82nd birthday.

ABOVE: A joyous family scene as the proud parents play with William. Both Charles and Diana remarked on being captivated by the new arrival – the young prince, meanwhile, is captivated with the toy rattle.

BELOW: Three-year-old Prince William sets off for his first day at nursery school, complete with a small flask of orange juice.

More sporting success followed at Ludgrove Preparatory School in Berkshire where he studied for five years. William was captain of the hockey and football teams and represented the school in cross-country running. It was while he was at Ludgrove that his parents announced their separation in December 1992.

The marriage of Charles and Diana had deteriorated steadily during the second half of the 1980s. Wendy Barry, the housekeeper at Highgrove, later recalled, "William was by now old enough to be aware of the rows and tensions in his parents' marriage. No amount of play-acting can ever fool a child."

The week before the announcement, Diana drove to Ludgrove to break the news of their parents' separation to her sons. William, although only ten, took the news stoically and said, "I hope you will both be happy now." Diana later reflected on her concerns for her eldest son: "He's a child that's a deep thinker and we won't know for a few years how it has gone in. But I put it gently without any resentment or anger."

Under the terms of the separation the two princes would now divide their weekends away between Diana at Kensington Palace and Charles at Highgrove House in Gloucestershire.

Weekends with the princess often involved treats – from burgers at McDonalds in Kensington High Street to white-knuckle rides at Alton Towers in Staffordshire. At Highgrove, William grew accustomed to country pursuits from an early age. The 348 acres of parkland were perfect for bike rides, skateboarding and riding his Shetland pony away from the prying eyes of the public. Later he enjoyed shooting and stalking with his father on the Queen's estates, as well as polo – Charles bought him a polo pony for his 17th birthday.

The family would put on a united front at occasional royal engagements, such as the anniversaries of VE Day and VJ Day in the summer of 1995. Also that September, Charles and Diana posed for photos

BELOW: Princess Diana and her two princes enjoy a splash on a water ride at the Thorpe Park amusement park in April 1993.

ABOVE: Prince Harry and Prince William stand betweent heir parents during the VJ Day commemorations staged outside Buckingham Palace in August 1995. The event, which marked the 60th anniversary of victory over Japan in the Second World War, was attended by 15,000 veterans and tens of thousands of spectators.

with their two sons when William arrived to study at Eton College.

In July 1997 a helicopter landed in the grounds of Kensington Palace to take Diana, William and Harry on what would turn out to be their final holiday together. Mohamed Al Fayed, the Egyptian-born owner of Harrods International, had invited them to stay on his yacht *Jonikal* which then headed for St Tropez where the family owned a villa.

It was during this cruise that Diana was introduced to Al Fayed's 42-year-old son, Dodi. The two began a highly publicized affair that tragically ended with their deaths in an horrific car crash in Paris just six weeks later.

The young princes were staying at Balmoral Castle with their father when Diana died. Both Charles and the Queen were woken in the early hours of the morning when news of the accident was forwarded from Buckingham Palace. The prince decided to let his sons sleep on until 7.30 when they normally awoke. Fifteen minutes later he went to their adjoining rooms to break the news to them that their mother was dead.

During the days that followed William and Harry showed remarkable self-control and maturity beyond their years.

Later in the week they again remained composed when they took flowers from well-wishers in the grounds of Kensington Palace.

The following day the two princes stood shoulder to shoulder with their father, their grandfather Prince Philip, and their uncle Earl Spencer when they walked behind their mother's coffin as it made its farewell journey through the capital.

Prince Charles now reconstructed his work and leisure time so that his world could revolve around his two young sons. The boys joined him in March

BELOW: Soldiers of the 1st Battalion, Welsh Guards carry Diana's coffin into Westminster Abbey for her funeral on 6 September 1997. Behind it walk Prince Charles, Prince Harry, Earl Spencer, Prince William and Prince Philip.

ABOVE: On a March 1998 visit to Vancouver, Canada, with his father and brother, William shows his impish side – having been presented with Canadian Olympic jackets and baseball caps, William decides to put his hat on back to front.

1998 for a visit to British Columbia in Canada during which William was given a rapturous welcome from thousands of Vancouver's teenagers.

In the summer of 1998 William passed nine GCSEs with A grades in English, History and Languages. He had already passed three others the previous year, and the royal family was said to be "privately delighted" that William had been so successful despite the trauma of his mother's death. The prince's A Level passes – an A grade in Geography, a B in History and a C in Biology – confirmed his status as one of the brightest royals. It also meant that he gained his university place at St Andrews on merit rather than favouritism.

Charles was keen that his son should take a year off before continuing his academic career so that he could see something of the world and take advantage of the fact that the media was so far respecting his privacy. He opted to join 15 other volunteers for a ten-week Raleigh International project in the remote community of Tortel, deep in the heart of the Andes. Here, he slept on the floor, cleaned the toilets, chopped firewood and made some "absolutely foul" porridge. TV coverage of the visit gave a glimpse of his natural affinity with children when he acted as a classroom assistant in a nursery school, and his six-year-old charges in turn leaped on his back and insisted he carry them around.

During his year off William also joined his father's regiment, the Welsh Guards, to take part in training exercises in the jungles of Belize. Then in September 2000 he headed for Mauritius to carry out an educational programme with the Royal Geographical Society.

Ironically, given the vast amount of travel and the exotic locations, William's favourite part of his year off was the short time he spent much closer to home. "The best bit was in England," he told a journalist before starting at university. "I loved working on a farm, before foot and mouth, which is why I've got so much sympathy for the farmers who have suffered so much from it. It was the best part of my year. I got my hands dirty, did all the chores, and had to get up 4.00 am. I got to see a completely different lifestyle."

Having stretched himself physically it was now time for William to resume his academic career. Aged 19, he said that he had little idea what the next four years would hold; he couldn't know that he was about to meet the woman who would one day become his wife.

2 CATHERINE MIDDLETON

The moment a royal engagement is announced, genealogists always scour their archives in an attempt to find a familial link between the two parties.

The results are often fascinating. Prince William's mother Diana, his stepmother Camilla and his former aunt Sarah, Duchess of York, are all descended from Charles II through some of his many illegitimate sons.

Kate's solidly middle-class background wouldn't automatically promise rich pickings for the researchers at the National Archives, but the more tenacious ones did find a link with Prince William. He and Kate are, it seems, related to Sir Thomas Leighton, an Elizabethan soldier, diplomat and for 40 years the Governor of Guernsey. He is the prince's 12th generation great-grandparent and Kate's 11th, making them 12th cousins once removed.

Kate and William are also both descended from King Edward III, famed for his crushing victory over the French at the Battle of Crécy in 1346.

Among Kate's other antecedents are Harriet Martineau, often cited as the first woman sociologist and the author of academic treatises such as *How to Observe Morals and Manners*. She also wrote allegorical novels including, to the delight of the researchers, *The Peasant and the Prince*.

OPPOSITE: On her first official appearance after their engagement was announced, Kate Middleton joined her husband-to-be at a charity event in Norfolk in December 2010 – all a far cry from the initial camaraderie that developed during their early days at university.

ABOVE: From Bradfield Southend the Middletons moved the short distance to Bucklebury. In recent times the royal connection has led to uniformed firearms officers brandishing semi-automatic machine guns patrolling the grounds.

Finally there are vague connections between other writers and Kate's family. She is a distant cousin of the children's author Beatrix Potter, and is also related to Arthur Ransome, who produced *Swallows and Amazons*. Ransome's sister Joyce was married to Hugo Lupton, the cousin of Kate's great-grandmother Olive.

The Luptons, Kate's ancestors on her father's side, were comfortably-off stalwarts of Leeds society in the late nineteenth and early twentieth centuries.

On her mother's side Kate's ancestors were of solid working-class stock. Take for instance James Harrison, who started work as a miner in the coalfields of County Durham in 1819, the year of Queen Victoria's birth. Generations of the family would work in the same profession.

The fortunes of Kate's family were to change again radically as recently as the 1980s thanks to the hard work of her parents. Michael Middleton is seven months younger than Prince Charles; Kate's mother Carole, born in 1955, is six years younger than her husband.

The couple had met in the 1970s when they both worked for British Airways (BA). Carole Goldsmith was an air stewardess and Michael was a flight dispatcher. His father Peter had been a pilot instructor, but Michael himself switched from pilot training to ground crew. His job was to co-ordinate the aircraft between arrival and departure – which involved everything from monitoring fuel intake to authorising take-off. He was the same grade as a captain and wore a similar uniform.

After dating for several years, the couple set up home in the Berkshire village of Bradfield Southend, some seven miles west of Reading. They married eight months later in June 1980 in the village of Dorney, with the 25-year-old bride arriving by horse and carriage.

Catherine Elizabeth Middleton was born on 9 January 1982 at the Royal Berkshire Hospital at Reading, coming into the world more than five months ahead of her future husband. She was christened at the fourteenth-century church of St Andrew's, near to the River Pang, and wore a traditional white gown. Afterwards, the family celebrated at the local manor.

Her younger sister Philippa, known as Pippa, was born at the same hospital 20 months later on 6 September 1985, and their only brother, James William, was born in April 1987 when Kate was five.

For the first 13 years of Kate's life the family lived in the village of Bradfield Southend. This is less than a ten-minute drive to where the Middletons live now, so Kate's home life for nearly 30 years has centred around the same four-mile area of Berkshire.

At the age of four Kate started at the local school, Bradfield Church of England Primary School, which was conveniently situated next door to the Middletons' home. Here, the future princess showed a healthy interest in sport – enjoying rounders, athletics and frequently swimming in the unheated outdoor pool, which she also used during her summer holidays. It was while she was at this school that Kate took her cycling proficiency test. She has remained a

ABOVE: During her time at St Andrew's School in Pangbourne, Berkshire, Kate excelled at a number of sports including tennis, swimming, netball, hockey and rounders. Kate, pictured in the middle of the front row, was the highest scorer on the under-12/13 rounders team.

keen cyclist ever since and was often spotted biking to lectures at St Andrews.

Michael Middleton was still working for BA, but Carole, with three children to look after, also found time to make party bags which she sold to other mums while Kate was still a toddler. This seed of an idea eventually germinated into Party Pieces which Carole founded around the time of James's birth "to inspire other mothers to create magical parties at home and to make party organising a little easier".

Kate's only written interview to date appeared briefly on the Party Pieces website in March 2010. Anyone logging on in the hope of hearing an exposé on her royal love life was disappointed, as her comments were confined to the party theme and her memories are as sugary as one of Carole's cakes.

In the autumn of 1989, Kate was sent to the co-educational St Andrew's School in Pangbourne, four miles from home. Again, she excelled at sport, winning swimming races and joining the netball team. She was also good at the high jump and broke the school record for her age group.

Kate was also keen on amateur theatricals, starring in the school production of the Tchaikovsky ballet *The Nutcracker* and taking the role of Eliza Doolittle in *My Fair Lady*. In her final year she starred as the heroine in a Victorian melodrama, which was videoed at the time and has since been on several TV documentaries mainly because her love interest in the play was called William. In one scene he falls to his knees and asks her to marry him. She replies, "Yes, it's all I've ever longed for. Yes, oh yes, dear William… Ah to think I am loved by such a splendid gentleman." Sadly, by the end of the play, the Pangbourne William had dumped her and her baby, and was never heard of again.

BELOW: Kate, pictured on the far left of this line-up, was a popular pupil at St Andrew's. It was at St Andrew's, as a ten-year-old, that she first saw William when, amid great excitement, the nine-year-old prince came to the school to play a hockey match.

By the time Kate was a teenager, Party Pieces was flourishing. In July 1995, when Kate was 13, the family moved to its present home on the outskirts of Chapel Row, in the parish of Bucklebury, a typical English village with a pub, tearooms and a village green.

The following April Kate arrived at Marlborough School, founded in 1843 in the Wiltshire town of the same name. Old Marlburians include John Betjeman, singer Chris de Burgh, Princess Anne's former husband Mark Phillips, the BBC's security correspondent Frank Gardner and, since Kate's time, Princess Eugenie.

The school had been fully co-educational for only six years, and Kate moved into the girls' boarding house, Elmhurst. What definitely appealed to her were the tremendous sports facilities.

Several friends from her Marlborough days have given newspaper interviews and none of them has a bad word to say about Kate. Kathryn Solari who

BELOW: At 13, Kate went to Marlborough School; a schoolmate has since revealed that Kate kept a poster of Prince William in her dorm room and said – perhaps in jest – that she would marry him one day.

studied biology with her recalls: "Catherine was always really sweet and lovely. She treated everyone alike. She was a good girl and quite preppy – she always did the right thing – and she was very, very sporty. I wouldn't say she was the brightest button but she was very hard-working."

Former classmate Charlie Leslie described Kate as "level-headed and down to earth". She said, "Kate is an absolutely phenomenal girl – really popular, talented, creative and sporty." One college master described her as an A-grade pupil and an all-rounder who was popular throughout the school.

Thankfully for Kate's present role, there seem to be few, if any skeletons in her cupboard. "I never once saw her drunk," recalls Jessica Hay.

She was similarly abstemious when it came to romance. The only name linked to her from her schooldays is fellow student Willem Marx, whom one school chum claims was "her first love", though Marx, now a 28-year-old journalist, steadfastly refuses to talk about any relationship they may have had.

Kate passed her 11 GCSEs with flying colours. She returned the following term to begin her A level studies and friends noticed a change that summer of 1998. "She came back an absolute beauty," remembers Gemma Williamson. "She never wore particularly fashionable or revealing clothes – just jeans and a jumper – but she had an innate sense of style."

Kate's time at Marlborough paid off and in her A Levels she gained A grades in Mathematics and Art as well as a B in English.

Like William, the next stage for Kate was a year off. Two months after graduating, she stayed in Florence where she immersed herself in the city's rich legacy of paintings and sculptures. After Florence, Kate joined Raleigh International, co-incidentally the same organization that William had joined. Like the prince, Kate went to Chile, though not on the same expedition; hers was in the spring of 2001, several months after William had returned.

ABOVE: Michael and Carole Middleton arrive at the Concert for Diana at Wembley Stadium in July 2007; Kate's parents set up a mail order firm, Party Pieces, in 1987 which, through the advent of the internet, became a huge success.

Malcolm Sutherland from Ross-shire, who worked for Raleigh International at the time, met them both and recalls, "For ten weeks each lived with absolutely no luxuries. This was roughing it by anyone's standards. Kate's trip involved three weeks of trekking, three weeks on a marine survey and her remaining weeks on a community.

"There was absolutely no connection between the couple at that stage and it's an incredible coincidence that they chose the same company and the same organization, but I think it shows how well suited William and Kate are."

Malcolm feels they will make a great couple: "She's an incredibly straightforward down-to-earth girl. I think she'd be supportive to William but not subservient. She's a modern girl, hugely intelligent and fun. I think she's exactly what the monarchy needs."

Kate's family tree with its emphasis on hard work, community service and moral integrity, down through the generations, has reached fruition in Kate. The confidence she gained from her close-knit family, her academic success, her love of sport and her faultless personality would all equip her to face her next stage in life – university.

BELOW: Kate's brother and sister, James and Pippa – seen here at an Issa show during London Fashion Week in February 2010 – both followed her to Marlborough College.

3 ST ANDREWS

"I just want to go to university and have fun," said 19-year-old Prince William as he prepared for four years of study at St Andrews, Scotland's oldest university. He added: "I want to go there and be an ordinary student. I mean I'm only going to university. It's not like I'm getting married – though that's what it feels like sometimes."

Ten years on, his words are ironic. Little did he realize back in 2001 that the path to academic success would also lead to the altar.

William had opted for the four-year History of Art course. The fact that his granny happens to own more than 7,000 paintings by Rubens, Titian, Vermeer, Gainsborough and so on, would after all give him a bit of a head start over his classmates.

With the approach of the start date, 23 September 2001, the prince became increasingly nervous. Prince Charles arranged to take him to college and on the way there they dropped in for lunch with the Queen Mother at Birkhall, her Deeside home.

The 101-year-old lady sensed that her great grandson was apprehensive and, kissing him a fond farewell, she joked, "Any good parties, invite me down!"

William had chosen St Salvator's Hall, or "Sallys" as he would soon call it, where he would stay for

OPPOSITE: The view over St Andrews town and the Cathedral ruins. Prince William and a certain Kate Middleton would be studying at the town's university until June 2005.

ABOVE: On his arrival at St Andrews, William was warmly greeted by an enthusiastic crowd – plus the inevitable bank of photographers.

OPPOSITE: Kate Middleton, a future flatmate of William but at this point dating a fourth-year student, evidently made her mark at the university fashion show of March 2002 with this daring outfit – a sheer black lace dress over a bandeau bra and black bikini bottoms.

the next year in a suite of rooms large enough to accommodate his ever-present security team.

Arriving at college is nerve-wracking enough for anyone, but to pull up outside his new hall of residence in the family car with 3,000 locals and 100 photographers watching his every move must have been mortifying for William. Blushing strongly and with his hands firmly rammed into the pockets of his faded denims, William looked awkward as the fans and well-wishers cheered his arrival. Prince Charles tried his best to dress down, wearing white slacks with brown suede shoes, though his double-breasted jacket with a pink silk hankie in the top pocket put him firmly in the "embarrassing Dads" category.

University is a great social leveller, and once he had dropped his royal title and became William Wales – or plain "Will" to his new mates – he soon melted into the background. Like the rest of the students he wore jeans, shirt and a jumper – or more often a fleece, to keep out those east-coast breezes.

Making friends when you are a prince isn't easy, though William was confident of his ability to gauge true characters amid the many new faces at St Andrews. "People who try to take advantage of me and get a piece of me I spot it quickly and soon go off them. I'm not stupid," he said.

No doubt he was as astute when it came to meeting women. During his time at "Sallys" William kept bumping into the same attractive brunette. Kate Middleton was more shy and demure than the other girls, though, to her embarrassment, she had already been labelled the prettiest girl at "Sallys" by the end of Freshers' Week.

Not only did they share the same hall of residence but they were also on the same course, and when there was a clash of timetable, Kate would take notes for Will and vice versa.

They had a great deal in common. For a start, they both shared a love of sport. Kate would get up early and be out jogging before breakfast, often arriving back just before the canteen closed. William timed his own breakfast to coincide and invited her to join his group. The pair shared a passion for swimming and would swim together most mornings at the luxury Old Course Hotel.

Although he and Kate were good friends, it was just a platonic relationship at the time, since Kate was dating Rupert Finch, a fourth-year student. However it was Kate who persuaded him to change his course to Geography and he felt relieved and happy with the switch.

It was during his second term that cupid's dart hit William one evening at the end of March 2002. It was the night of the annual Don't Walk charity fashion show at the five-star St Andrews Bay Hotel.

The prince had paid £200 for his front-row seat and his eyes nearly popped out of his head when Kate walked down the catwalk wearing a see-through dress and black underwear.

Afterwards, there was a party at 14 Hope Street, a student house, and William made his move, engaging Kate in a long conversation and leaning in for a kiss. Kate who was still dating Rupert, rebuffed him.

William had to bide his time and, for the time being, they remained just good friends. This was still the case in September of that year when Kate, Fergus Boyd and

ABOVE: Graduation day delight! Kate's four-year university course culminated with a 2:1 degree in Art History and she and William both graduated on 23 June 2005.

Olivia Bleasdale moved into a shared flat with the prince at 13a Hope Street. The four of them paid £100 a week rent and shared the cooking and cleaning.

At some point in the next few months Kate and William became a couple, though they went to elaborate lengths to hide it, arriving and leaving the flat and lecture halls separately, and never holding hands or going to parties together.

Although the couple were happy to stay in watching DVDs or ordering takeaways, they would go out with friends to the West Port bar on South Street or to Ma Bells, where many students met, beneath the Golf Hotel on the Scores. Then there was the Lizard on North Street, where they could enjoy a late night dance or two.

At the start of their third year, William and Kate moved to Balgove House on the Strathtyrum estate, a four-bedroomed cottage about a quarter of a mile out of town, which offered them more privacy.

William and Kate's four-year university course ended in June 2005 when the couple graduated at the same ceremony, William with a 2:1 degree in Geography and Kate with a 2:1 in Art History. Charles and Camilla, who had been married at the Guildhall

in Windsor just two months earlier, were present along with the Queen and Prince Philip. For the Queen, it was an opportunity to catch her first glimpse of the girl who had captured her grandson's heart.

William and Kate and the royal party listened to the words of the Vice-Chancellor, Dr Brian Lang, at the end of the ceremony. "You will have made life-long friends," he told the graduates. "You may have met your husband or wife. Our title as the top matchmaking university in Britain signifies so much that is good about St Andrews, so we rely on you to go forth and multiply."

We now know at least one couple took him at his word.

ABOVE: Prince William acknowledges the crowd after graduating at St Andrews in June 2005. As one chapter of his life closed, another was not only gathering pace but getting the thumbs-up, too.

OPPOSITE: The Queen and Prince Philip join the newly wed Duke and Duchess of Rothesay for Prince William's graduation ceremony at St Andrews in June 2005.

4 A LOW-KEY COURTSHIP

Kate's daring catwalk appearance in March 2002 had made William sit up and take notice of his friend, but it would be a while before romance blossomed.

In the autumn of the same year, Kate was one of a party of 16 friends, including the prince, who stayed at Wood Farm on the Queen's Sandringham estate for a shooting weekend. Long-lens photos of the group taken by local photographers show Kate wreathed in smiles standing next to the prince. It was the first time that the couple had appeared in the same frame and inevitably fuelled speculation that this young lady was "the one".

In May 2003 the couple were again snapped unawares, this time they were deep in conversation at a rugby sevens match. The same month Kate's father gave a good-natured rebuttal to a journalist's suggestion that his daughter might be dating the future king. "I spoke to Kate just a few days ago," said Michael, "and I can categorically confirm they are no more than good friends."

Michael added, "We're very amused at the thought of being in-laws to Prince William, but I don't think it's going to happen."

A month later, William celebrated his 21st birthday with an "Out of Africa" themed party at Windsor

OPPOSITE: William and Kate show a rare display of public affection at an Eton College Old Boys Field Game in 2006.

ABOVE: Kate and her mother Carole show their support for Prince William during a polo game on a windy summer's day in Tetbury, Gloucester, in 2005.

OPPOSITE: Princes William and Harry take to their skis in Klosters, Switzerland, with Kate in March 2005. The inclusion of William's girlfriend on this break fuelled the rumours of an imminent royal engagement.

Castle. His uncles, Earl Spencer and the Duke of York, were dressed as big-game hunters and his grandmother was dressed as her African counterpart the Queen of Swaziland, complete with tribal headdress. "I thought it would be fun to see the family out of black ties and get everyone to dress up," he told an interviewer a few days earlier.

After the Windsor party the prince took the unusual step of denying the romance with Jecca. His spokeswoman announced, "St James's Palace denies that there is or ever has been any romantic liaison between Prince William and Jessica Craig."

In an interview to mark his milestone birthday, William flatly denied that romance was on the horizon with Kate... or anybody else. "There's been a lot of speculation about every single girl I'm with, and it actually does quite irritate me after a while, more so because it's a complete pain for the girls....

"If I fancy a girl and she fancies me back, which is rare, I ask her out. But at the same time, I don't want to put them in an awkward situation, because a lot of people don't understand what comes with me, for one – and secondly, if they were my girlfriend, the excitement it would cause."

The exact date when William and Kate's friendship developed into a romance remains uncertain, though it is thought to have been some time towards the end of 2003.

It was the following Easter, in April 2004, that it became obvious they were a couple. Paparazzo Jason Fraser, who had broken the news of the Diana and Dodi romance by photographing them kissing on the Al Fayed yacht *Jonikal*, snapped a series of photos of William and Kate in a chairlift at the ski resort of Klosters. The couple are staring fondly at each other and the next morning's *Sun* newspaper carried the photo and the headline: "FINALLY... WILLS GETS A GIRL".

Two weeks before the wedding of Prince Charles to Camilla Parker Bowles, William and Harry had returned with their father to Klosters for a genteel

on the morning of her birthday a few days later there were dozens outside, eagerly awaiting a timely announcement. For William it was all too reminiscent of the hounding his mother had received in the run-up to her marriage, and his office issued a statement condemning the harassment Kate was receiving. "He wants more than anything for it to stop," said his Press Officer. "Miss Middleton should, like any other private individual, be able to go about her everyday business without this kind of intrusion. The situation is proving unbearable for all those concerned."

William was now based with the Household Cavalry at Combermere Barracks in Windsor. There were the occasional meetings with Kate in London, however, by now much of the spark had gone out of the relationship.

ABOVE: Kate stands out from the crowd at William's Passing Out parade at Sandhurst in December 2006. Now that he had graduated from Sandhurst, the question on everyone's minds was, would she still be "Waity Katie"?

OPPOSITE: William shares a joke with his grandmother as The Queen inspects his Passing Out parade at the Royal Military Academy, Sandhurst, in December 2006; Kate, her parents and brother Jamie were also guests at the graduation ceremony.

LEFT: Kate lets her hair down, but keeps up appearances leaving the high-end Mahiki nightclub, London in February of 2007 wearing a knee-length printed silk dress by New York designer BCBG Max Azria.

ABOVE: Demure rather than dashing, Kate and Prince William go through the motions at the Cheltenham Festival of March 2007; this was the last time the couple were pictured together before it emerged that they had separated in mid-April.

Their attendance at the first day of the Cheltenham Festival on 13 March 2007 which would prove to be the last time they were photographed together in public until later in the summer. While Kate managed a forced smile, William looked distinctly out of sorts.

Three days later, William moved to Dorset to begin a ten-week tank-commander course at Bovington army training camp.

The couple's last meeting together after this was during the Easter weekend when they finally decided to call it a day. News of the break-up appeared in the tabloids on Saturday 14 April and the same day Kate was photographed looking tense and drawn as she walked from the car into her parents' house.

In previous generations when the royals split from a partner, there would be no contact afterwards. This period in their relationship, unsurprisingly, seems to have had a profound effect on them, and they spoke about it openly and at length during their interview with Tom Bradby on the day of their engagement. Kate admitted that she had been angry about it at the time but she said that she now looked back on it as a positive experience and admitted she had been "consumed" with the relationship.

The newly single William wasted no time in hitting the nightclubs again, enjoying a late night drink at Bliss wine bar in Bournemouth and, on the eve of the story breaking in the newspapers, he was at Mahiki, in London's Mayfair, one of his favourite haunts.

BELOW LEFT: Life goes on – Prince WIlliam heads away from his brother's leaving for Iraq party at the end of April. Prince Harry had been scheduled for deployment to the front line within weeks, a decision that was subsequently reversed for safety reasons.

BELOW RIGHT: Looking crestfallen, Kate walks back into her parents' home in Bucklebury, Berkshire, the day after her split with Prince William was announced on 14 April 2007.

Meanwhile Kate may have been angry, but she wasn't about to mope. The week after the split, she and her mother Carole went to Dublin to attend a private exhibition of paintings by Gemma Billington, in the Hanover Quay area of the city. They also toured the National Gallery of Ireland.

Back in England, she herself took onto the London nightclub scene. Always friendly and polite to the press, she seemed to be making more of an effort than ever to co-operate, with the result that the photos of her splashed across the papers were of a carefree, happy and undoubtedly sexy girl about town.

Kate also made headlines when she took part in a new charity venture with the Sisterhood, a group of 21 girls who aimed to row a Dragon boat from Dover to the French coast to raise money for charity.

By now, she had resumed her affair with William, although it wasn't common knowledge. The first the world at large knew of the rekindled romance was at the Concert for Diana, held at Wembley Stadium on 1 July 2007 on what would have been William's mother's 46th birthday. Kate and William sat two rows apart and never exchanged a glance during the evening – but at the after-show party they were inseparable. A snatched photo of them taken with a mobile phone shows them deep in conversation, over a candle-lit supper. The message was clear: the romance was back on.

BELOW: Prince William, sitting in the front row alongside his brother, is two rows away from Kate (far right, in conversation with her brother James). William and Kate barely exchanged glances during the six-hour music extravaganza, but were inseparable at the after-show party.

Any doubts that the royal romance was back on were dispelled later in the month when Kate was invited to Camilla's 60th birthday party at Highgrove.

Camilla had been keen to invite her all along as she had always got on well with Kate, but it had to be William's decision in the end. The prince was adamant that she should be there but he was equally determined not to upstage his step-mother's big day. Kate wore a stunning full-length cream dress and appeared happy and relaxed as she sipped champagne in the beautiful gardens.

Ironically, the same month that she was the belle of Camilla's ball, Kate was named the most sought-after party guest in town by *Tatler*. It was also during this year that Kate began to receive plaudits for her

fashion sense, and there were, and continue to be, obvious parallels drawn with the woman who would have been Kate's mother-in-law. In July 2006, UK *Vogue* editor Alexandra Shulman wrote, "Kate is a contemporary version of Princess Diana. She has the same mainstream style and will go on like Diana to get more glamorous."

For the House of Windsor, it is a plus that Kate also plays it safe in the sartorial stakes. Her style is as discreet as her personality: attractive, classy, always appropriate for the occasion and with just the hint of quirkiness.

In August 2007, the couple holidayed on Desroches Island, in the Seychelles. It was an opportunity for the two to be alone – apart from the inevitable personal detectives – in what would be their

OPPOSITE ABOVE: The photo that proved that William and Kate were back together. Pictured here in Windsor Great Park on a pheasant shoot – a Christmas gift from the Queen – the couple were later seen hugging and kissing.

OPPOSITE BELOW: William becomes the latest member of the royal family to earn his Royal Air Force "wings". Kate joins him at the graduation ceremony in Lincolnshire in April 2008. The previous day William attended the 90th anniversary dinner of the RAF.

LEFT: William towers over his father at an RAF wings Graduation Ceremony in April 2008 – at 6 ft 3 in William would be the tallest-ever British monarch.

first overseas holiday since January 2006. Here, it is reckoned that the couple made a pact. Kate needed reassurance that the romance was going places, and William needed to know that he could concentrate on his career – he still had to spend another six months' deployment with the RAF and the Royal Navy. Marriage would be on the cards, but it would be a way off yet.

William and Kate reached an "understanding" on the holiday that marriage would definitely take place, though as we now know, the actual date would be a fair way down the line.

ABOVE: A rare photo of Kate kissing and cuddling her prince after a romantic meal at the Potting Shed Pub in Wiltshire in July 2009 – not surprisingly such intimacy led to further speculation about the pair's future plans.

RIGHT: Happy and relaxed: William and Kate take a stroll at Coworth Park, Ascot in May 2009; the couple enjoyed a post-match drink after William and his brother Harry had played polo.

OPPOSITE: On the final day of his unofficial visit to Australia in January 2010, Prince William arrives at Government House to a mass of adoring fans and wannabe princesses – it was the first time William had returned to Australia since going there with his parents when he was just nine months old.

During the spring and summer of 2008, Kate attended four high-profile events in relatively quick succession that left no one in doubt that her position as royal girlfriend was definitely that of a princess-in-waiting, a phrase that began to be used time and again.

On 11 April she made her first appearance at a royal engagement since William's Sandhurst graduation 16 months earlier. On that occasion she hadn't been photographed together with the prince. Now she was filmed walking through RAF Cranwell side by side with him. It was presumed that she would attend the event, although her name was not on any official operations notes beforehand, and she slipped in through a private entrance with William's aunt, Lady Sarah McCorquodale.

Peter Phillips's wedding a month later, on 17 May, was Kate's second high-profile event. Nearly all the royal family were present at St George's Chapel, Windsor, although one significant absentee was

BELOW LEFT: A solemn-looking Kate leaves her London flat in July 2007 on her way to work at Jigsaw; at the time she and William were not together.

BELOW RIGHT: A cheerful Prince William greets Naval families in Churchill Square, Helensbrough, Scotland.

William who honoured a long-standing commitment to attend a wedding in Kenya

Another month on, and Kate was present, again at St George's Chapel, to watch the procession of garter knights walk from the state apartments of Windsor Castle and through the Lower Ward to the chapel. The Order of the Garter is Britain's oldest order of chivalry and William was greatly touched that his grandmother had made him the 1,000th knight.

Kate's fourth royal event was another wedding. Lady Rose Windsor, the 28-year-old daughter of the Queen's cousin, the Duke of Gloucester, married George Gilman at the Queen's Chapel, next to St James's Palace on 19 July. Kate looked cool and elegant in a light-blue jacket complementing her multi-coloured silk skirt. In her long flowing hair she wore a black fascinator, that mainstay of modern royal headgear. Once again William was absent, this time on board HMS *Iron Duke* on patrol in the Caribbean, as a part of his five-week placement with the Royal Navy.

It had been speculated that William would leave the armed forces in 2009 to become a full-time working royal. In September 2008, Clarence House issued a surprise announcement that the prince intended to train with the RAF Search and Rescue. The course would last 18 months and, if he successfully qualified, he would be committed to serve a unit for three years. The prince's office was keen to point out that he would also still work for the charities and organizations with which he was involved and that he would also undertake some royal duties.

While the prince's future was being mapped out, there was still no sign of his girlfriend pursuing a long-term, challenging career. She had quit her job as an accessories buyer for fashion chain Jigsaw in November 2007 after working there for less than a year. The Queen, 85 in April 2011, still undertakes almost 400 engagements a year and was reportedly concerned that Kate was giving herself a work-shy image. By early 2009 Kate was working for the family

ABOVE: Remembrance Sunday 2007 sees Prince William placing a wreath at the Cenotaph in Whitehall for the first time, a sign of his deep respect for the military.

ABOVE LEFT: In an outfit that would surely impress Her Majesty, Kate attends the August 2009 wedding of Captain Nicholas Van Cutsem and Alice Hadden-Paton at The Guards Chapel. William also attended and was teasingly told, "You'll be next!"

ABOVE RIGHT: In a stunning floor-length dress by London design house, Issa, Kate attends the Boodles Boxing Ball in London, in support of Starlight Children's Foundation.

OPPOSITE: William and Harry visit the Semonkong Children's Centre in Lesotho. Following in their mother's footsteps, the princes are showing an increased interest in charity work.

business, Party Pieces. She was reportedly training in website design and launching a new promotion called First Birthdays. It helped to offset some of the criticism that she wasn't the highest of achievers, career-wise, and more importantly it gave her time off whenever William was free to meet her.

William began his training at RAF Shawbury, in Shropshire, on 11 January 2009, two days after he enjoyed a birthday dinner and farewell party rolled into one at the Middletons' home. The sightings of William and Kate were getting fewer and fewer. However, 2010 would finally provide the royal news that so many people had begun to suspect would never happen.

5 THE ENGAGEMENT

On 15 January. Kate was in the audience at RAF Shawbury to see William receive his certificate for successfully completing his advanced helicopter-training course from his father Prince Charles. She rose to her feet and applauded enthusiastically when the prince's name was announced.

In his speech, Prince Charles spoke about the dangers facing a search and rescue pilot as well as poking fun at some of the less onerous tasks: "Some of you no doubt will find yourselves in Afghanistan where the ground troops will put great faith in you.

"Others no doubt among you will be plucking people from danger, maybe sheep in distress, not to mention endless ladies with conveniently sprained ankles on awkward mountainsides across the country."

Later in the month Flt Lt Wales arrived at RAF Anglesey to start his training, hoping to become a fully operational pilot by the summer, having learned the skills required to operate Sea King Helicopters.

Meanwhile, the prince also took another important step forward in his apprenticeship as monarch when he represented the Queen at the opening of the new £38-million Supreme Court in Wellington during a five-day visit to New Zealand. It was to be his first official overseas trip and he told officials it meant "an awful lot" to him.

OPPOSITE: Although they actually got engaged in October 2010, Kate and Prince William chose 16 November to announce the news to the world.

OVERLEAF: Royal grandeur: the world's press gather for a photocall in the State Rooms of St James's Palace as Prince William and Kate Middleton announce their engagement in November 2010.

As the couple began discussions for the wedding preparations, their first join engagements were arranged. As with his father before him, William found himself showing his fiancée the ropes as they made their first public appearance at a charity fundraiser for the Teenage Cancer Trust in Thursford in Norfolk just before Christmas 2010.

In February, their next engagement took place much closer to "home" as the couple headed for Trearddur Bay on Angelsey, not far from RAF Valley where Prince William is based, to launch a new RNLI lifeboat. Both had the opportunity to practise their Welsh as they joined in the Welsh national anthem and a hymn. Then further engagements took them to Belfast on 8 March and back to where it all began – St Andrews. There, the crowd's greetings made them feel, as William put it, as "if we were coming home". In honour of their wedding, the university had created a

BELOW: Kate and William admire a gift from the RNLI which commemorated their visit to Trearddur Bay.

OPPOSITE: William and Kate pose for the press as they are greeted by dignitaries on their visit to Belfast on 8 March, which happened to be Shrove Tuesday and thus gave them both the chance to try their hand at tossing pancakes.

ABOVE: Dressed in a bright red suit, Kate watches Prince William as he makes a speech at their alma mater, St Andrews University.

OPPOSITE: Prince William offers advice as his fiancée signs the Book of Condolence at the New Zealand High Commission on 25 February 2011.

scholarship, and William made a speech as patron of St Andrews' 600th anniversary appeal.

Following a tour to New Zealand and Australia to offer his sympathies after the earthquake in Christchurch and the flood disasters in Queensland, Prince William flew back to join Catherine and his brother, Prince Harry, at the New Zealand High Commission to sign a book of condolence for the victims of the earthquake.

William and Catherine' last engagement before the wedding took place in Lancashire on 11 April. In spite of the rain, they received what William described as a "warm Lancastrian welcome" when they arrived to open the Darwen Aldridge Community Academy. Wearing a dark blue suit and looking very slim, Catherine sheltered under an umbrella, while William ignored the raindrops. Appearing happy and relaxed, they greeted well-wishers and William spoke at the Academy, telling his audience, "I know that I am very fortunate. I have the support of my family and friends, I do a job I enjoy … and I have Catherine."

6 THE WEDDING

For the past eight years it was talked about, analysed and predicted and, on 29 April 2011 it finally came true.

The wedding of Prince William of Wales, second in line to the British throne, and his long-time love, Catherine Middleton, took place at Westminster Abbey with all the pomp and pageantry that Britain loves and does so well.

It might not have been the state occasion that Charles and Diana's wedding was, but the difference was barely noticeable, since this royal union caught the public's imagination as much as that of William's parents. Media coverage of the preparations for the marriage of William and Catherine sent the national psyche into overdrive and for one glorious day this spring, at a time of war and economic crisis, good news for once dominated the front pages.

William and his Kate managed to keep much of their relationship under wraps. For the past three or four years the only time we seemed to see them was at the weddings of their friends, many of them from the couple's days at the University of St Andrews.

Those weddings nearly always followed the same pattern: a service in a quintessentially medieval parish church, a reception in a nearby manor house or stately home and, of course, a couple of long lenses

LEFT: William and Kate leave Westminster Abbey as husband and wife.

ABOVE: Prince William greets members of the crowd waiting outside Clarence House on the night before the wedding.

OPPOSITE ABOVE: The Mall leading up to Buckingham Palace decorated with British flags in the days leading up to the wedding.

OPPOSITE BELOW: Spectators started gathering outside Westminster Abbey days before the actual wedding.

poking through the hedge. William and Kate were said to have longed for the same low-key ceremony surrounded by just family and close friends, but they recognized that as a future king and queen they had an obligation to share their wedding day with the nation. Their medieval church needed to be Westminster Abbey, dubbed "the parish church of England". Their stately home would be the 1,000-roomed mansion at the end of The Mall and this time a couple of thousand long lenses were on hand to document every second of the day.

In the months following their engagement, the couple managed to keep a large part of their wedding plans a secret. The most talked about royal wedding dress of the decade, as well as the name of its designer, stayed under wraps and we were not even told where it was being made. Despite the Abbey being one of the most popular tourist attractions, William and Kate also managed to attend a couple of rehearsals without being spotted, even though Kate on one occasion arrived with her sister Pippa, Prince

Harry, four bridesmaids and two pageboys.

William later admitted at the very end of March that "the whole thing" of his wedding was already giving him sleepless nights with four weeks still left to go. He said, "I did a rehearsal the other day and my knees started tapping quite nervously, so it's a daunting prospect and very exciting."

The bridegroom-to-be was "very pleased" that both he and Kate had managed to hold a stag do and hen party without the press knowing. Details were not released, but William would only say that Harry organized his "like a military operation", and guests at both were sworn to secrecy. It was all a far cry from the last royal stag weekend, that of William's cousin Peter Philips, which was described as a 72-hour bender on the Isle of Wight. During it the group managed to lose Peter and in the words of Harry it "was an awesome stag do – it will just take us a while to recover".

William offered to work with his Search and Rescue team right up until his wedding day, but spent his last night as a single man at Clarence House with

his brother in the apartments that they will share with Kate after the wedding. At the last two major weddings held in the capital, both Diana Spencer and Sarah Ferguson also stayed at Clarence House, which was then occupied by HM Queen Elizabeth the Queen Mother. At the Windsor wedding of Prince Edward, his bride Sophie Rhys Jones, spent the eve of her wedding at another of the Queen Mother's homes, the Royal Lodge in Windsor Great Park, and six years later Camilla Parker Bowles stayed at the castle itself before her civil ceremony at the Windsor Guildhall in 2005.

Kate, however, broke with tradition and decided to spend her last night as a commoner at the Goring Hotel in Belgravia. The 101-year-old hotel is literally just over the garden wall of Buckingham Palace and is often used as an annexe for the palace when large parties of guests are in London for major events. Shortly before the wedding, the hotel's present owner, Jeremy Goring said, "We are delighted we are going to play a small part in what's going to be a great day of celebration around Britain," adding that "primarily the

ABOVE: Two young spectators waiting for a glimpse of William and Kate.

BELOW: A family from Dartford in Kent camp out the day before the wedding.

Goring is a hotel that makes people feel at home".

Kate, together with her sister Pippa and her brother James, stayed there with their parents, Carole and Michael, on the eve of the wedding. The bride-to-be occupied a five-room apartment on the fifth floor of the hotel, which was upgraded in the aftermath of the announcement of the engagement. Kate's luxurious Royal Suite boasts a dark-wood, four-poster bed, a grand piano, a waterproof TV in the bathroom and an original "Venerable" lavatory by 19th-century plumber Thomas Crapper – the supplier of loos to several royal households.

One fitting that was removed just before Kate arrived was a white bridal gown and coronet of flowers that is believed to be a prototype of Queen Victoria's wedding dress. It normally stands in a glass-fronted wardrobe next to the bed Kate slept in, but perhaps the sight of a marriage gown wasn't thought to be the best thing to lull her to sleep the night before her wedding. One artefact that did stay was a painting of the television character Blackadder, who was played by

ABOVE: The international media building that was constructed opposite Buckingham Palace.

Rowan Atkinson, kissing the hand of Queen Elizabeth I.

While Kate spent a sedate evening with her family at the Goring, William and Harry shared a brotherly dinner at Clarence House with the Prince of Wales and the Duchess of Cornwall before they stepped outside to thank people in The Mall, who had come to wish them well, for their support. Meanwhile, the Queen and the Duke of Edinburgh together with various members of the world's royal families dined in splendour at the Mandarin Oriental Hotel in Knightsbridge, opposite Princess Diana's favourite store, Harvey Nichols. Besides most of the British Royal Family, guests included Queen Margrethe of Denmark, King Harald of Norway, Prince William's godfather, the exiled King Constantine II of Greece and Prince Albert of Monaco and his fiancée Charlene Wittstock.

Many members of the public had camped out on folding chairs or in tents in the key positions along The Mall overnight. Others had already staked their places opposite Westminster Abbey days before in sleeping bags, huddling under blankets as the temperatures dropped after a warm Easter the previous weekend.

A vast, glass-fronted, three-storey press area was

built at Canada Gate to offer numerous TV and radio crews a bird's-eye view of Buckingham Palace and crucially its famous balcony, where the bride and groom would appear after the wedding and share an obligatory kiss. Film crews from around the world had gathered in London, not only those you would expect from Commonwealth countries, but others from as far afield as Mexico, Brazil, Poland, Russia and China. One flustered organizer estimated that, without a single member of the public, either side of the 987-metre long Mall could be entirely filled by members of the media. To save the public purse, member of the press and their organizations had to pay for positions on the stands, with the prime spot opposite the palace costing £1,000 per person while a photographer standing opposite the Abbey had to pay £650.

OPPOSITE: An aerial view of the crowds in Whitehall.

BELOW: Crowds line the streets of Whitehall on the wedding day.

As dawn broke over London, below stairs at the
Goring Hotel, the staff were already at hard at work
ensuring that anything Kate and her family needed was
ready and to hand. The last royal bride to be married
at Westminster Abbey, Sarah Ferguson, recalled her
pre-wedding preparation at Clarence House: "In the
middle of breakfast the troops began rolling in: the
hairdresser and manicurist and beautician, with Lindka
Cierach [her wedding dress designer] on hand to advise
on the make-up to best complement my dress, and my
Mum was there for moral support."

Even the bubbly "Fergie" admitted to nerves, and it
would only be natural for Kate to have had butterflies
in her stomach as she faced her last family breakfast
as a Middleton. With her mother Carole and Pippa on
hand to calm her nerves, Kate also had her "troops" to
rely on. First on the scene was her hairdresser, James
Pryce, senior stylist for Richard Ward, whose task was
to ensure the bride's trademark shiny, lustrous hair was
as shimmering and sleek as we've grown accustomed
to. True to her trademark style, Kate kept her hair

ABOVE: A cheering crowd waiting to see William and Kate pass by on their way to Westminster Abbey.

LEFT: An aerial shot of the thousands of people who gathered in London's Hyde Park to watch the wedding on huge screens.

ABOVE: Earl Spencer with his Canadian fiancé Karen Gordon standing amongst the congregation.

LEFT: Tara Palmer-Tomkinson, standing next to her sister Santa, wearing a striking, electric blue dress and Philip Treacy hat.

ABOVE British film director Guy Ritchie and his girlfriend Jacqui Ainsley.

OPOSITE BELOW: Sir Trevor Brooking and his wife Lorna wearing a stunning purple outfit.

RIGHT: David and Victoria Beckham wait together with other guests queuing to get into the Abbey.

ABOVE: Princes William and Harry, the groom and best man, in their Bentley on their way to the Abbey.

OPPOSITE: Princes William and Harry arrive at Westminter Abbey, smiling at the crowds as they go in. Prince William was dressed in the scarlet uniform of the irish Guards of whomhe is an honorary colonel.

Other celebrity names included Sir Clive Woodward, the former English rugby coach, Sir Trevor Brooking, Ben Fogle and the comedian Rowan Atkinson. Madonna's former husband, the film director Guy Ritchie, was also invited and happens to be Kate's sixth cousin once removed.

Six royal ex-partners were among the couple's personal guests. They included Rupert Finch, whom Kate dated at St Andrews in her first year and Willem Marx, a friend from her Marlborough College days whom she was rumoured to have dated while in the sixth form.

ABOVE: Queen Sonja of Norway waving to the crowds as she walks into the Abbey.

ABOVE RIGHT: Crown Princess Victoria of Sweden and her husband Prince Daniel standing on the red carpet.

Arabella Musgrave, who dated William the summer before he went to St Andrews, was invited, along with William's first girlfriend Rose Farquhar. Isabella Anstruther-Gough-Calthorpe, whom William is said to have pursued during the summer of 2004, was also present and Jecca Craig, who was reported to be his first true love, arrived with her boyfriend Captain Philip Kaye. William is particularly close to the Craig family and has stayed with them several times in Kenya. Jecca's parents, Ian and Jane were invited as was her brother Batian and his wife Melissa. William was asked to be best man to Batian and such was his regard for the family that the prince attended the Craig wedding rather than that of his cousin Peter Phillips which was held the same weekend.

Other names from William's past included Olivia Hunt, who attended Edinburgh University with Kate's sister Pippa. A former member of the Beaufort polo set, Natalie Milbank was invited with her husband Ed and Davina Duckworth-Chad, once named as a potential bride for William, was there with her husband Tom Barber.

There were 15 members of Kate's family present with probably the most controversial being her uncle Gary Goldsmith, who made tabloid headlines when he allegedly sold drugs to an undercover reporter and

ABOVE: Prince Albert II of Monaco and his fiancée, the Olympic backstroke swimmer, Charlene Wittstock.

LEFT: Spain's Queen Sofia, Crown Prince Felipe and Crown Princess Letizia.

ABOVE: Queen Margrethe II of Denmark

RIGHT: Prince Alexander and Princess Katherine of Serbia

boasted that William and Kate had stayed at his luxury home in Ibiza during a summer break. As Carole's only brother his presence was never in doubt and he attended with his former wife Luan and their ten-year-old daughter Tallulah.

Michael and Carole were allocated 100 tickets to distribute to family and friends. They invited the chairman of Reading FC, John Madejski, who lives near the family in Berkshire, and the Tory MP Richard Benyon and his second wife Zoe.

Like his great aunt Princess Margaret before him, William has fallen in love with the Caribbean island of Mustique and a number of guests associated with the island were also invited, including John and Belle Robinson who own the villa on the island in which

the prince and his then girlfriend holidayed. The Robinsons own the high-street chain Jigsaw for which Kate was an assistant buyer for a short time at the end of 2006. Other guests present met either William at Eton or Kate at Marlborough, or both of them at St Andrews. Some, such as nanny Barbara Barnes, who looked after the prince as a child, had known William all his life.

Most of the guests sat in either the nave of the Abbey or one of the two transepts – in the north and south of the sides of the great church, where they could see the service on a series of large television monitors. Only relations, close friends and foreign dignitaries sat in the quire area where the actual service took place. Afterwards, many guests commented

ABOVE LEFT: Ex-King Constantine of Greece with his wife, Queen Anne Maria.

ABOVE RIGHT: Grand Duke Henri and Grand Duchess Maria Teresa of Luxembourg.

ABOVE: Lady Helen Taylor and her husband Timothy Taylor arrive for the ceremony.

RIGHT: Princesses Beatrice and Eugenie arrive outside Westminster Abbey for their cousin's wedding.

LEFT: Lord and Lady Frederick Windsor. Lord Frederick married Sophie Winkleman in September 2009.

ABOVE RIGHT: Zara Phillips, MBE poses for photographs with her fiancé Mike Tindall. This was one of the first high-profile royal events that the couple had attended since the announcement of their engagement.

on the overwhelming fragrance of the spectacular flower arrangements that decorated the Abbey and the spectacular "living avenue" of maple trees which lined the nave. The aisle was also decked with symbolic native flowers grown on the Highgrove estate. According to Shane Connolly, the couple's "floral designer", Kate told him that "it has to be British". Connolly added, "Catherine is a dream client... like few other brides I've ever met. She has an incredibly

honour to be asked to do such a fantastic event and use some amazing flowers as well."

The Abbey itself was looking its finest, thanks to the work of Vanessa Simeoni, the Head of Conservation, and her team who had ensured that everything – from brass plaques to the various artworks – was carefully cleaned ahead of the big day. This included a last-minute vacuuming of the blue-carpeted nave.

Sharing the quire area with the guests was the Choir of Westminster Abbey under the direction of James O'Donnell, the organist and choirmaster, who worked with William and Kate on their choice of music, which they had planned by late February.

O'Donnell told reporters that the choir is consistently trained to a high level so that when services like the royal wedding come along they are prepared: "Yes this is an enormous occasion. But the way to approach it, I believe, is as one would approach any sung service: you have to keep your act together." On the day itself, he also directed the Choir of the Chapel Royal which combined with his own choir to create a truly memorable effect. The choice of music reflected a very British theme with compositions by William Walton, Edward Elgar and Sir Peter Maxwell Davies.

While the press and public waited the arrivals, the main topic of conversation for both was the title granted to the couple by the Queen. It had been suggested that the Queen might break with tradition and grant permission for Kate to be known as Princess Catherine, but in the end it was announced at 8.00 am that Prince William had been given the titles of

OPPOSITE: Her Majesty Queen Elizabeth II is greeted by the Very Reverend Dr John Hall, Dean of Westminster.

BELOW: Kate's sister and maid of honour Pippa leaves the Goring Hotel in London with two of the younger bridesmaids. Pippa's elegant white dress was also designed by Sarah Burton for Alexander McQueen.

Duke of Cambridge, Earl of Strathearn and Baron
Carrickfergus, the latter two titles giving him links to
both Scotland and Northern Ireland. Thus, Catherine
Middleton would henceforward be known as HRH
The Duchess of Cambridge.

At 9.50 am the first of the diplomatic corps arrived.
According to protocol, the Governors-General and
Prime Ministers of what are quaintly called "realm
countries", such as Canada, Australia and New Zealand
are invited to this kind of high-profile royal event.

The leaders of Britain's three main political parties
were also invited together with their partners. All three
wore morning suits, which they donned in an apparent
U-turn after it was widely reported that they would be
wearing lounge suits.

At slightly after 10.10 am a Bentley emerged
through the gates of Clarence House and into Stable
Yard Road before taking a sharp left into The Mall.

*OPPOSITE: Pippa Middleton
guides the four younger
bridesmaids and two pageboys
into Westminster Abbey.*

*ABOVE: Guests stand for the
entrance of the Queen and the
Duke of Edinburgh.*

LEFT: The Prince of Wales and the Duchess of Cornwall followed by the Queen and the Duke of Edinburgh process through the quire of Westminster Abbey to their seats near the high altar.

ABOVE: Kate travels through London on her way to Westminster Abbey with her father Michael Middleton.

Princes William and Harry were on their way to the Abbey some 45 minutes ahead of the bride. It was a poignant reminder of that September morning, 14 years earlier, when as two sorrowing sons they followed the body of their mother on its final journey through London and on to her funeral at Westminster. In an interview to mark the tenth anniversary of Diana's death, William said, "There isn't a day that goes by without we don't think about her," and his wedding day would almost certainly be no exception.

As the two brothers arrived at the Great West Door at 10.15 am, they were met by the Very Reverend Dr John Hall, who was installed as the 38th Dean of Westminster in December 2006. As the Abbey is what is known as a Royal Peculiar, he answers only to the Queen. Assisting him on the day was his verger, Martin Castledine, who walked ahead of the Dean carrying a silver mace.

ABOVE: The Prince of Wales takes a moment to look back down the aisle for a glimpse of the bride's arrival.

LEFT: Carole Middleton chats to relatives as they wait for the wedding ceremony to begin.

Shortly before the wedding, Dr Hall talked about his role on the day: "I will be conducting the service; welcoming people at the beginning, introducing the service and giving the blessing at the end." He added that everyone at the Abbey was "very excited about it and are working pretty hard to make sure it's the most wonderful occasion".

A few minutes later, members of numerous foreign royal families arrived together on a coach. Again protocol dictates that the only foreign heads of state who attend a royal wedding are from monarchies or Commonwealth countries, so the widely expected invitation to President Obama never materialized, though he was due to visit the UK anyway just four weeks later.

ABOVE: Designer Sarah Burton for Alexander McQueen fixes Kate's dress as she and her father Michael enter Westminster Abbey.

LEFT: The crowds get their first proper view of Kate Middleton in her wedding dress designed by creative director of the Alexander McQueen label Sarah Burton. According to a press release from St James' Palace, Kate selected the British brand because of the "beauty of its craftmanship and its respect for traditional workmanship".

ABOVE: An aerial view of the bridesmaids and pageboys waiting for the ceremony to begin emphasises the simple design of the bridesmaids' dresses.

OPPOSITE: Michael Middleton leads his daughter down the aisle, followed by her attendants.

FOLLOWING PAGES: Michael and Kate Middleton process past the choir as they sing Parry's "I was Glad".

Royal reunions are also family affairs because Elizabeth II, her fellow Queen, Margrethe of Denmark, and the Kings of Norway, Sweden and Spain are all great great grandchildren of Queen Victoria who was dubbed "the Grandmother of Europe". Prince William would not have attended the weddings and funerals of foreign royals, though this will inevitably change once he becomes Prince of Wales and eventually king.

At 10.20, Carole Middleton, dressed in a sky-blue coat and dress ensemble created by the designers at Catherine Walker, and her son James left the Goring Hotel. It must have been an emotional wrench leaving her daughter behind as she began the seven-minute journey to the Abbey. Both she and Michael have

ABOVE: Prince William was seen to say "You look beautiful" to Kate as her father brought her to William's side.

OPPOSITE: Michael Middleton, Kate and William sing the first hymn of the service "Guide me, O thou great Redeemer".

grown to love William as their own son and the prince calls Kate's father "Dad". Neither parent had any concerns about the compatibility of the young couple, but at the same time they couldn't help but feel some concern about the role their eldest daughter was taking on, which had catapulted her onto the world's stage, like Diana before her.

After Carole left for the service, Kate still had her sister Pippa on hand to dispense some sisterly words of love and support and, of course, as maid of honour, to look after the other attendants. With the other four bridesmaids all aged between three and eight, Pippa must have had her work cut out

looking after them and the pageboys. The bridesmaids were Lady Louise Windsor, the seven-year-old daughter of Prince Edward and his wife Sophie; Margarita Armstrong-Jones, aged eight, the daughter of the Queen's nephew Viscount Linley; Grace van Cutsem, the daughter of Hugh and Rose van Cutsem, who is also William's goddaughter and finally Eliza Lopes, the Duchess of Cornwall's three-year-old granddaughter. The two pageboys were William Lowther-Pinkerton, the ten-year-old son of William's Private Secretary James Lowther-Pinkerton and Master Tom Pettifer, aged eight, whose mother "Tiggy" Pettifer, née Legge-Bourke, was hired as nanny to William and Harry after their parents' separation.

As Pippa Middleton ushered the four small bridesmaids into the car that would take them to the Abbey, it was just possible to see their ivory-coloured, box-pleated, ballerina-length dresses, which had been

OPPOSITE: Prince William and Kate exchange vows.

ABOVE: Prince William takes Kate's right hand and places a wedding ring which is made of traditional Welsh gold on her fourth finger.

ABOVE: Spectators wearing Union Jack hats and Kate and Willam shawls outside the Abbey.

RIGHT: Crowds in Trafalgar Square watch the ceremony on big screens surrounding Nelson's Column.

created using the same fabric from which the bride's dress was made. English Cluny lace was just visible underneath the skirts and the dresses were finished with pale gold silk sashes. Unlike the bride's dress and that of her sister, Pippa, the bridemsaid's dresses were designed by Nicki Macfarlane.

The two pageboys wore uniforms in the style of those worn by Foot Guards officers during the Regency period in the 1820s. The vivid red tunics with their

ABOVE: The couple are amused as William's attempts to place the wedding ring on Kate's finger aren't immediately successful.

gold braiding provided a lovely bright splash of colour.

Pippa, as the only adult attendant, wore a simple sheath dress in a heavy, ivory, satin-based crepe with a cowl neckline and button and lace details that mirrored those of the bride's dress.

While Carole and James Middleton made their way to their seats to the left of the altar in the area known as the Sacrarium, the British royal family arrived. The Queen's Gloucester and Kent cousins and other more distant relatives came by motorcoach, followed by cars carrying Prince Andrew and his daughters Beatrice and Eugenie, the Earl and Countess of Wessex and the Princess Royal and her husband Vice-Admiral Tim

ABOVE: Now married, the Duke and Duchess of Cambridge, as they will be known, sat for the reading of the lesson and the address.

Laurence. For both Andrew and Anne, the day must have recalled their own weddings in the same location, both of which started with such high hopes and only to end in separation and divorce. Prince Charles and the Duchess of Cornwall arrived next followed three minutes later by the Queen and Prince Philip, who as sovereign and consort still take precedence over the father of the groom.

The Queen was dressed in a primrose-yellow dress and coat made out of crepe wool with a matching hat, all of which were designed by Angela Kelly. The Duchess of Cornwall wore a champagne-coloured dress and over that a two-toned coat in champagne

and duck-egg blue, which was created by Anna Valentine.

Finally, at shortly after ten minutes to eleven, the moment so many millions were waiting for around the globe finally arrived as Kate and her father left the Goring Hotel, giving everyone their first glimpse of the bride on her wedding day.

A covered walkway hid the dress as Kate climbed into the Silver Jubilee Rolls-Royce, so that only glimpses of it would be caught as she and her father made their way down The Mall and across Horseguards Parade before turning into Whitehall. It could only be seen in all its splendour as she arrived at the Abbey. This time there was no repeat of Diana's wedding when her taffeta dress emerged crumpled

ABOVE: The Right Reverend Richard Chartres, Bishop of London gives the address to the congregation watched by the Duke and Duchess of Cambridge and members of the clergy of Westminster Abbey.

OPPOSITE: Kate's brother James Middleton reads the lesson, which was taken from Romans, Chapter 12, verses 1, 2 and 9–18.

FOLLOWING PAGES: A bird's-eye view shows the couple kneeling at the high altar for the closing prayers of the ceremony.

from the Glass Coach. As Kate alighted from the Rolls-Royce just after 11 o'clock, there was a cheer from the thousands of well-wishers who had camped out all night on Victoria Street and Broad Sanctuary just to witness this moment.

Made of ivory and white satin gazar, it was said that Kate wanted a dress that reflected British craftsmanship. The lace appliqué work on the bodice and skirt was done by the Royal School of Needlework and used a technique known as Carrickmacross that

OPPOSITE: William leads his wife out of the Edward the Confessor Chapel after the signing of the register.

ABOVE: After making their bow and curtsey to the Queen, the new husband and wife walk past the royal family as they leave Westminster Abbey.

ABOVE: The wedding party walk through the avenue of trees lining the aisle leading up to the altar. In total, six field maples and two hornbeams were placed in Westminster Abbey.

OPPOSITE: William and Kate emerge through the Great West Door of Westminster Abbey together.

originated in Ireland in the 1820s. Individual flowers were hand-cut from lace and laid onto ivory silk tulle to create an organic effect. The skirt was designed to reflect an opening flower and flowed out behind the bride in a train that at its longest measures 2 metres 70 centimetres. The back of the dress was finished with 58 gazar and organza-covered buttons, while the underskirt was also made of silk tulle trimmed with Cluny lace.

On their arrival, Kate and her father Michael were greeted by Dr Hall as they made their way to the Great West Door. For many royal brides, this is the most daunting moment when hundreds of faces crane round to see them as they are framed against the huge glass doors. It is also the moment for the bride's father to offer a few words of comfort and support. At Princess Margaret's wedding, Prince Philip gave away the bride.

As they waited for the procession to begin, he said to the princess, "I don't know who's more nervous, you or me!" He then asked, "Am I holding onto you, or are you holding on to me?" The bride whispered, "I'm holding on to you!" Michael Middleton and his daughter no doubt exchanged similar nervous asides.

Then, as the organ began to play and the choir sang the opening words of Parry's "I was Glad", the bride's procession began and Kate and her father walked through the nave packed with hundreds of friends from school and university as well as their social set. Arm in arm, they continued through the flower-decked

ABOVE: Following the wedding, Michael and Carole Middleton talk to Prince Charles and the Duchess of Cornwall as they wait for their carriage.

OPPOSITE: William and Kate wave to the crowds waiting for their first glimpse of the newly-married couple.

archway under the organ loft and emerged into the quire where William with a smile on his face caught the first glimpse of the woman he was about to marry.

The Dean of Westminster Abbey, Dr John Hall welcomed the congregation with his opening words and then handed over to Dr Rowan Williams, the Archbishop of Canterbury, for him to perform the marriage ceremony. In clear voices, William and Kate made their vows. After the singing of the hymn "Love Divine, All Loves Excelling", a lesson from the New Testament was read by Kate's brother James and then an anthem especially composed for the occasion by John Rutter with words from Psalm 118 was sung by the choirs.

The address that followed it was given by the Bishop of London, Dr Richard Chartres, who is a close friend of the Prince of Wales from when they were both at Cambridge University. The bishop confirmed Prince William and was one of the executors of Princess Diana's will, and delivered the address at her memorial service in 2007. In September 2009, he officiated at the wedding of Lord Frederick Windsor to Sophie Winkleman at Hampton Court Palace. The bishop spoke of how everyone shared in the couple's joy and how successful relationships allowed each partner space and freedom. He closed with a prayer that the couple had composed themselves which asked that "in the busyness of each day" the couple's eyes should be "fixed on what is important in love" and that they be helped to "be generous" with their "time and love and energy".

During the service, music was provided by the 39 musicians of the London Chamber Orchestra (LCO) who were based in the organ loft that separates the quire and nave. The LCO was conducted by its musical director, Christopher Warren-Green, who has performed at several concerts for the royal family.

The signing of the register by the bride and groom took place in private in the Edward the Confessor Chapel witnessed by Prince Charles, the Duchess of Cornwall, Carole and Michael Middleton and

OPPOSITE: Carole Middleton with the Queen and the Duchess of Cornwall outside Westminster Abbey following the ceremony.

ABOVE: The Prince of Wales and Michael Middleton look over at the crowds who had gathered outside the Abbey.

FOLLOWING PAGES: From left: the Earl of Wessex, the Duchess of Kent, the Countess of Wessex, the Princess Royal, Vice-Admiral Timothy Laurence, Viscountess Linley, Princess Alexandra and the Duke of York.

PREVIOUS PAGES (LEFT): The Duke and Duchess of Cambridge begin their carriage procession to Buckingham Palace, passing the Houses of Parliament.

PREVIOUS PAGES (RIGHT): The couple wave to the crowds who patiently waited to see them following their marriage.

ABOVE: Prince Harry in the carriage procession with Lady Louise Windsor and Tom Pettifer. Eliza Lopes, the granddaughter of the Duchess of Cornwall is also in the carriage, but not shown here.

Kate's sister, Pippa. Then, as man and wife, William and Catherine returned to the Sacrarium while the trumpeters from the Central Band of the RAF, under the direction of Wing Commander Duncan Stubbs, played a fanfare specially composed by Stubbs. Called *Valiant and Brave* the 30-second piece announced to the world that William and Kate were now man and wife.

When William and Kate emerged from the chapel, they made their way down the steps from the high altar and stopped to bow and curtsey to the Queen before making their way down the aisle, smiling at the congregation as they did so.

As William and Kate emerged from the Abbey, a peal of bells signalled the end of the service. Outside, the crowds cheered and shouted good wishes as the couple slowly climbed in to the 1902 State Landau that had also carried William's parents from their wedding at St Paul's.

The five-carriage procession left Westminster at 12.15. Following the bride and groom were the bridesmaids, pages, Pippa Middleton and Prince Harry, with the Queen and Prince Philip in the fourth carriage and Prince Charles, the Duchess of Cornwall and Mr and Mrs Middleton in the fifth. Accompanying them was a detachment from the Household Cavalry that William joined in September 2006 as a lieutenant following in the footsteps of Prince Harry who had joined the previous January. Smiling and waving, William and Kate looked happy and relaxed as their carriage entered Parliament Square before journeying along Whitehall, across Horse Guards Parade and

BELOW: Excited well wishers walk behind the police towards Buckingham Palace to celebrate the royal wedding.

PREVIOUS PAGES: Crowds with banners surge towards Buckingham Palace, hoping to see the happy couple on the balcony.

ABOVE: The wedding party gathers on the balcony of Buckingham Palace to wave to the excited crowds.

OPPOSITE: William and Kate share a kiss to the joy of those watching below.

into The Mall before reaching Buckingham Palace 15 minutes later. For the thousands that had slept out or waited since dawn it was at long last a chance to see the bride and groom, and to welcome Britain's future queen.

Once all the carriages and mini coaches carrying the other members of the royal family had arrived at the palace, the crowd was slowly brought down The Mall by the police and thousands gathered outside the palace awaiting the balcony appearance shortly after 1.25 pm when they were rewarded with not one but two versions of what has become the traditional kiss between the bride and groom. A few minutes later, the newlyweds were honoured with a flypast by the RAF and the Battle of Britain Memorial Flight that included a Lancaster, a Hurricane, a Spitfire, two Typhoons and two Tornado GR4s.

LEFT: The newlyweds and crowds ouside Buckingham Palace are honoured with a flypast by the RAF.

ABOVE: Planes from the RAF's flypast soar above the crowds of spectators whose numbers were so great that they stretched back down The Mall.

ABOVE: The Duchess of Cambridge meets the Governor-General of Canada, HE The Rt Hon. David Johnston and Mrs Sharon Johnston.

Inside the palace, a reception for 660 people got underway in the State Apartments while the official photos were being taken by Hugo Burnand. The Queen had entrusted her cousin once removed, Lady Elizabeth Anson, and her Party Planners company with the task of creating the perfect party. The palace chef, Mark Flanagan and his team, produced a variety of savoury and sweet canapés for the event. The couple then cut the wedding cake created by the Leicestershire-based cake designer Fiona Cairns. Its cream-and-white icing was covered in flowers at the bride's request who chose them according to the messages that they represented. In addition, William asked McVitie's to create a chocolate-biscuit cake made from a Royal Family recipe, one of his personal favourites.

Music for the event was provided by Claire Jones, the Official Harpist to the Prince of Wales. Speaking

before the reception, Claire said, "I have performed
for Prince William before – both privately and on a
rugby pitch in 2008 – but I've never met Kate. It will
be lovely to; I'm very excited and absolutely honoured.
I'll be looking for something special to wear. This is an
historic occasion and truly a dream come true."

After the reception, hosted by the Queen, a more
élite gathering of 300 was entertained to a dinner
hosted at the palace by the Prince of Wales, who
asked the legendary chef, Anton Mosimann, to cater
for the event. Then, after the Queen and Prince Philip
retired to bed, the palace was turned into a nightclub

*BELOW: Prince William greets
The Hon. Julia Gillard, the
Australian Prime Minister, at
the first reception after the
wedding ceremony.*

and reverberated with the sound of a DJ and decks, complete with a dance floor, lights and a cocktail bar.

William and Kate very much wanted to create a wedding day that was personal to them as well as satisfying the need to hold this most private of events in front of millions of onlookers in London and billions of people around the world. As the party died down and the last palace light was switched off, they could be satisfied that it was a personal as well as a national triumph.

OPPOSITE: The eight-tiered wedding cake, decorated with 900 delicate sugar-paste flowers was created by cake-maker Fiona Cairns.

BELOW: Prince William and Kate drive away from Buckingham Palace in Prince Charles' dark blue Aston Martin.

PUBLISHERS' ACKNOWLEDGEMENTS

The publishers would like to thank Michael Jermey and
Mike Blair at ITV News and Kevin Morgan at ITV for their
help in the production of this book.

PICTURE CREDITS

Images were supplied by the following:

Alamy/StockImages
Getty Images
Press Association Images
Rex Features
Solo Syndication

Every effort has been made to acknowledge correctly and
contact the source and/or copyright holder of each picture
and Carlton Books Limited apologises for any unintentional
errors or omissions, which will be corrected in future
editions of this book.

PUBLISHERS' CREDITS

Editorial Manager: Vanessa Daubney
Editors: Jenifer Barr & Victoria Marshallsay
Art Director: Lucy Coley
Design: Barbara Zuniga
Jacket Design: Alison Tutton
Picture Research: Steve Behan
Production Manager: Maria Petalidou